Stories from Faiths
Buddhism

The Sound the Hare Heard
and Other Stories

Copyright © 2007 QEB Publishing

First published in the United States by
QEB Publishing, Inc.
23062 La Cadena Drive
Laguna Hills, CA 92653

www.qeb-publishing.com

Library of Congress Control Number: 2007001012

ISBN 978 1 59566 378 8

Written by Anita Ganeri
Design and editorial by East River Partnership
Illustrated by Laure Fournier
Series Consultant Roger Butler

Publisher Steve Evans
Creative Director Zeta Davies
Senior Editor Hannah Ray

Printed and bound in China

The Sound the Hare Heard
and Other Stories

Anita Ganeri

Illustrated by Laure Fournier

QEB

Birth of the Buddha

Long ago, a king and queen lived in a splendid palace. One night, the queen dreamed that she saw a white elephant with a flower in its trunk.

The queen wanted to know
what the dream meant. She
sent for some wise men. They
told her that she was going
to have a very special baby.

Soon, the time came for the baby to be born. The queen set off for her father's house in the next kingdom. This was the custom at that time.

On the way, the queen
stopped to rest in a beautiful
garden. It was filled with
flowers, fruit trees, and
butterflies. And there,
her son was born.

The gods scattered rose petals over the baby. The trees suddenly burst into bloom. Then, a great earthquake shook the ground, for this was no ordinary baby.

8

The queen took the baby back to the palace.
The king was overjoyed to see them. He threw
a great party to celebrate his son's birth.

One day, a wise man
visited the palace.
He told the king and
queen that their son
would grow up to be
a great ruler or a
very wise teacher.

The king and queen named their son Siddhartha, which means "the one who makes wishes come true." Later, he became a wise teacher and people called him the Buddha.

Siddhartha and the Swan

Siddhartha grew up in his father's palace. He was kind and caring to everyone. He especially loved the animals that lived in the palace gardens.

12

One day, Siddhartha was sitting by the lake. He looked up at the sky. A flock of beautiful white swans was flying by above his head.

Suddenly, one of the swans
fell from the sky. It landed at
Siddhartha's feet. Siddhartha
saw that an arrow was stuck
in the swan's wing.

14

Siddhartha wanted to take care of the swan. Very gently, he pulled out the arrow. Then, he wrapped the swan in his shawl to keep it warm.

15

Just then, Siddhartha's cousin came rushing up. His name was Devadatta. He told Siddhartha that he had shot the swan, so it belonged to him.

16

Siddhartha did not want to give up the swan. The two boys quarreled and quarreled. In the end, they asked a wise man to decide who should have the swan.

The wise man told them this.
The swan belonged to the boy
who tried to save its life, not to
the boy who wanted to harm it.

So, Siddhartha kept the swan and cared for it until it was better. Then he took the swan to the lake and let it fly away with its friends.

19

The Generous Prince

There once lived a prince named Vessantara. He was famous for being very generous. In fact, he was so generous that he kept giving his belongings away.

The prince even gave away his great white elephant
to the people in the next kingdom. The elephant
was the most precious thing that the prince owned
because it had the power to make the rain fall.

Many people in the prince's kingdom were angry with him for giving the elephant away. They thought that their kingdom would have no rain. So, the king sent the prince away to live in the forest with his wife and children.

One day, an old holy man came
walking by. He asked the prince to
give him his children to be his servants.
The generous prince was very sad, but he
was so generous that he agreed to let them go.

Not long afterward, the holy man came back again. This time, he asked the prince for his wife. Again, the prince was very sad, but he was so generous that he agreed to let her go, too.

But, the old holy man was actually
the god Lord Indra in disguise.
He had heard about the prince. He
wanted to find out for himself just
how generous the prince really was.

Lord Indra was very impressed that the prince was
so generous and that he did not think of himself.
He brought the prince's wife and children back.
They were overjoyed to see each other again.

In time, the people forgave Prince Vessantara.
He was allowed to go back home. The king was
so pleased to see him that he decided to give
up his throne and make the prince king instead.

The Sound the Hare Heard

One day, a hare was sitting under a fruit tree when he had a terrible thought. What if Earth fell to pieces? What would happen to him?

Just at that moment, there was a gigantic CRASH! The hare jumped into the air. Then, he ran out of the forest as fast as he possibly could.

On the way, he met another hare who asked him what was wrong. "Earth is falling to pieces," the first hare cried. "Run for your life!"

Next, the hare met a deer and a tiger
and an elephant. Then, he met a
buffalo and a rhinoceros. The hare
told them that Earth was falling to
pieces. They all ran after him.

A wise lion heard the commotion. He asked the foolish animals why they were running away. They told him what the hare had said.

The lion was puzzled. There had not been an earthquake. The hare must have heard another sound. With a loud roar, the lion told the animals to stop. Otherwise, they would run into the sea and drown.

The lion ran back to the fruit tree and looked around. Earth was not falling to pieces. The sound that the hare heard was just fruit falling to the ground! The animals were safe.

In this story, the foolish animals believed what the hare had said. They did not think for themselves. Luckily, the wise lion was able to save their lives just in time.

Notes for Parents and Teachers

About Buddhism

Buddhism began in what is now the country of Nepal, between India and China, about 2,500 years ago with the teachings of a prince called Siddhartha Gautama, who later became known as the Buddha. Buddhists use his teachings as a guide for living their lives. Siddhartha saw that there was suffering and unhappiness in the world and set out to find a way of ending it. He left his privileged lifestyle behind to look for answers. He became the Buddha, the enlightened or awakened one, when he finally realized the truth about human existence. For the rest of his life, he traveled around India as a wandering monk, teaching people a path to follow to find happiness and leave suffering behind.

About the stories in this book

In each of the world's faiths, stories play an essential part. For centuries, they have been used to teach people about their faith in an accessible way, making difficult ideas and concepts easier to understand. For children in today's multicultural society, these stories also provide an ideal introduction to different faiths, their key figures and beliefs.

Birth of the Buddha

The story of the birth of the Buddha is a very important one for Buddhists. It is the story behind the key Buddhist festival of Wesak, which falls at the time of the full moon in April or May. Some Buddhists also commemorate the Buddha's enlightenment and death at Wesak. Buddhists decorate their homes and temples with lights, which symbolize the Buddha's enlightenment. These lights illuminate the darkness, just as the Buddha's enlightenment dispels ignorance and lights up the world.

Siddhartha and the Swan

The story of Siddhartha and the swan illustrates the key Buddhist teachings of karuna (compassion) and metta (loving kindness). These teach that Buddhists should respect all living things and not do anything to harm them. All Buddhists promise to live by five precepts, which together demonstrate compassion. It is not enough not to harm living things. We should actively show compassion and kindness.

The Generous Prince

The story of Prince Vessantara is found in one of the Jatakas—a collection of 547 stories about the past lives of the Buddha. Each story shows the Buddha, in the guise of a man or an animal, teaching important values such as friendship, compassion, and wisdom. In *The Generous Prince*, the Buddha appears as Prince Vessantara, a man of supreme generosity and selflessness. For Buddhists, these are two highly valued qualities.

The Sound the Hare Heard

In *The Sound the Hare Heard*, another Jataka story, the Buddha appears as the lion who saves the animals from certain death. The animals listen to rumors and unfounded fears rather than finding out the truth for themselves. If it were not for the lion's wisdom and compassion, they would all have rushed into the sea and drowned. Buddhists compare the lion's roar to the Buddha's teachings, which wake up the unenlightened.

Further things to do

• Read the stories to the children. Talk about the stories with them. Ask some questions about what the stories mean to them. For example, why did the Buddha leave his life of luxury behind? How did Prince Vessantara feel about giving away his children?
• Relate the stories to experiences in the children's own lives. For example, have they ever followed what someone said without really thinking about it, just like the animals that followed the hare? Or have they ever been very generous to one of their friends?
• Use a variety of different ways to tell the stories. Children could act out the stories, making masks and costumes for their characters to wear. Alternatively, you could make and use finger puppets from felt or paper.
• Decorate the classroom or home for Wesak. Make paper lanterns and lotus flowers. Talk about the meaning of the festival and of Buddhist symbols, such as the white lotus flower. The growth of this pond plant symbolizes a journey—the progress of the human soul from "muddy" materialism, through the "waters" of experience into the "light" of wisdom. Encourage children to make their own Wesak cards. Extend this activity to investigate other Buddhist festivals and the stories behind them.